I0541749

CATCH THEM YOUNG

A Key To Winning Children To Christ
"Book For Every Home"

Proverb 22:6

CATCH THEM YOUNG

A Key To Winning Children To Christ
"Book For Every Home"

Proverb 22:6

BY REV. DR JOHN AKINYEMI

ARPress

ILLUMINATING IDEAS
EMPOWERING VOICES

Copyright © 2022 by Rev. Dr. John Akinyemi.

All rights reserved. No part of this publication may be reproduced, distributed, or transmitted in any form or by any means, including photocopying, recording, or other electronic or mechanical methods, without the prior written permission of the copyright owner and the publisher, except in the case of brief quotations embodied in critical reviews and certain other noncommercial uses permitted by copyright law. For permission requests, write to the publisher, addressed "Attention: Permissions Coordinator," at the address below.

ARPress
45 Dan Road Suite 5
Canton MA 02021

Hotline: 1(888) 821-0229
Fax: 1(508) 545-7580

Ordering Information:
Quantity sales. Special discounts are available on quantity purchases by corporations, associations, and others. For details, contact the publisher at the address above.

Printed in the United States of America.

ISBN-13:   Softcover   979-8-89389-999-3
            eBook   979-8-89389-998-6

Library of Congress Control Number: 2024918085

"A KEY TO WINING CHILDREN FOR CHRIST BOOK FOR EVERY HOME"

TABLE OF CONTENTS

PREFACE

How can I raise my kids in such a world? How can I bring him up to do right and serve God in a world that is increasingly becoming more accepting of sin? A world that not only accepts sin but celebrates it.

But secondly, we should do more than just raise our kids to know God and to do what is right. That's just the start of it. That's only the base.

After teaching our kids who God is and the right way they should go, we should train them to be Kingdom Warriors. We should teach them not to be Christian bystanders, watching others take on all the risks and do the entire Kingdom work.

We should show them how to be active participants in the battle to win souls.

We need to teach our children to work hard for the glory of God. However, there are some things we can begin to teach our children now to prepare them for this life of independence.

Well, we can start by simply doing our part. God has given us a very special role in our kids' lives. He trusts us to steward them through this life.

So here are 6 ways we can start to do our part in stewarding our little ones:

1.   Pray over them. Pray over your kids. And I mean really pray. It's easy to remember to pray for the basics: protection, safety, health. And these are, of course, great things to pray for. But I say take it deeper. The enemy is prowling. And the minds of our children can be easy prey if we allow it. God put these babies in our care. And not just physically. Let's be intentional about covering our children in serious prayer.

Some examples:

o   Pray for their spiritual gifts to be manifest!
o   Pray that they will resist the devil!
o   Pray that they will walk by faith and not by sight!
o   Pray for their spiritual discernment!
o   Pray for their future spouse!

•   Speak over them. Much like prayer, where we ask for the grace of God to cover them, we should decree and declare God's promises over their lives. Don't just ask but declare in the name of Jesus.

• Monitor what they watch and listen to. Let's be diligent about protecting our children's eye and ear gates. Keep as much evil from their sight as early as possible. Guard their minds. Even something that seems harmless can spark an innocent curiosity that the enemy can use later

Below I've put together a list of 9 things we can teach our children to do for themselves to prepare them for spiritual battle.

Teach them HOW to pray, not just TO pray.

Teach them how to be THINKERS, so they aren't easily influenced.

Teach them how to LOVE, as defined by scripture.

Teach them to STUDY the Bible, and not just brush over the words.

Teach them what it means to WORSHIP, so they connect with God.

Teach them to PRAY DEEPLY, and not just recite cute poetry prayers.

Teach them how to FAST and why it's important.

Teach them to SEEK God diligently, in both good and hard times.

Teach them how to SERVE others with a generous heart

DEDICATION

This Book is dedicated to my Parents for their effort in training me in the ways of the Lord at my younger age.

Also, to my wife Beatrice Akinyemi for joining hand with me to train our Children in the way of the Lord, so also to our Children for allowing us to train them just with the way our Parents trained us, Glory to God all of us are enjoying our lives in God today.

INTRODUCTION TO THE BOOK

For over fifty years ago, myself and my wife Beatrice had been deeply committed to the Church work we help start both in Nigeria and America, both of us has served in numbers of capacities as lay leader and minister. My wife has always been with the children class as a teacher all along even up until date.

I believe in the local church. But many local churches are facing challenges, including the serious needs of families. That's why this book addresses ways to help build godly homes especially children.

Being the Pastor of a local church is one of the more difficult, tasking, and challenging job a person could ever undertake in life. The average layperson cannot fathom the expectation Pastors face from members of their congregation. From children to elderly care. From a hospital room, where a baby has just been born, to some homes where conflicts or disagreement is ongoing.

The spiritual and emotional weight of leading and loving a flock of believers is an awesome burden. They face discouragement as they see the messes some people have made of their marriages and their families.

I have three objectives in this book. The first is to encourage church leaders and children's teachers on how best they can teach young one for them to understand their messages, secondly for parents to stand up to the work of feeding their children with the words of God also teach the children about evangelism and for them from their youth to take winning soul as a matter of important.

I pray that we will see God working in the levies of our children like never before. Amen.

FOREWORDED BY PROF. JOEL ADEDEJI

Textbooks on Children Evangelism are hard to find. It is unusually takes for granted that children do not require a special approach to minister to them.

It is comfort to know from this book by Rev. (Dr. John Akinyemi) that an effective break through can be.

Is intrusive to be aware of the poser which Jesus Christ presents, "Suffer the children to come unto me, and forbid them not; experience pain in the Kingdom of God "means to experience pain in the attempt to bring about changing the disciples who had rebuked those who had brought the little children unto Him.

In His show of displeasure and outright condemnation of the attitude of the disciples, Jesus went on to enjoin them to "suffer "in the attempt to bring them to Him. Dr. Akinyemi has thrown a challenge to Bible teachers that evangelizing among children requires a method of approach which is distinct from the old Sunday school approach of making fables and stories of the Bible in order to bring out the trusty in the word of God to the children. Reaching out to the truth, according to Rev.Akinyemi, one needs the guidance of the Holy Spirit under special anointing to bring children into Christ.

In this book we realize that children are a hidden treasure of God, regarded highly by Jesus Christ because they are reserved as special herded for the kingdom of God, Rev Akinyemi has fashioned out an exciting and entertaining, but a studious approach carefully shaped on the anvil of experience as a teacher. Dr Akinyemi says, for example, "It is not enough to read to children from the Bible but there is a need to know what to put in a Biblical story or passage to make it a lesson "This is the crux of this book.

I recommend this book and that the approach worked out be prayerfully pursued and used for gain.

Children from a vital link to the body of Christ in the heavenly places far above all powers and principalities, it is the triumphant Church to bring them along without let or hindrance, and together, march from glory to glory. This book is the challenge, let us utilize its resource and bless Rev. Akinyemi for his epoch –making effort.

CHAPTER ONE
CHILDREN EVANGELISM

If we want to work in evangelizing children, then we must have Biblical bases for doing so. Therefore lectures/training will be divided into two.

(1) The Biblical bases for child evangelism
(2) The ways of evangelizing children

1. Bases for Children Biblical Evangelism

Without Biblical bases and assurance there is no way of evangelizing the child. Mark 16:15 was among the very last words of the Lord Jesus Christ to the disciples (including us– present day Christians) what was the command?" Go ye into the entire world and preach the gospel to every creature "It is a fact that not all can become Evangelist, Pastor or missionaries and "go into the entire world.....................but we can go through prayer; giving, full time ministration etc.

Children evangelism is not a ministration of telling stories, it is preaching the gospel. The verse quoted is a command to preach to all "creatures". This should not be disregarded in evangelism. They are not to be gathered aside as nuisance during church meetings leaving them in the hands of people who will tell those fables and stories. Rather, they are to be evangelized. Many of the children are demon-possessed. For example, when Jesus was coming down from the mountain where The Bible he was transfigured, he met his disciples inane attempt to cast a demon out of a boy (Matthew 17: 14-21, Mark 9:14-29) after reprimanding them about their faithlessness, Jesus asked the father of the boy when the demon came into him., and the father answered them "Of a child ("Mark 9:21)

The Bible enjoins us to "train up a child in the way he should go; and when he is old, he will not depart from it (Proverb 22:6)

When the men out of twelve sent to spy out the land of Canaan gave a bad report that made the children of Israel to grumble. The anger of God was kindled on them and

1

He vowed that the elders who saw all His acts in the wilderness would not get to Canaan, but the little ones. (Their children) whom they were grumbling would be destroyed would get into the land. (Number 13:26, 14:3, 14:26 -33)

After they perished the children were to be taught the commandments and covenants in Deuteronomy 5:1-3. The fathers died but the children raise up in their stead were to harkens and obey the commandments and covenants. Deuteronomy 6:7-8. Moses the man of God tells us of the laws and covenant of God while sitting down, standing, lying down, walking etc. Psalm 78:4-7 says the word of God must not be hidden from children. For example, a sister's son who has just come to live with a family, talks a great deal about farming methods, production of food crops such as yam, rice etc. He has been taught these things, despite the fact that he is still in primary care. One can imagine if this boy had been taught the word God like this, it is sure that he would have become a giant. We bless God; it is nevertheless not too late.

The consistent Christian has an unmatched opportunity to train children. Two of your children will not be alike and hence cannot be treated alike. As we proceed with these lectures we shall learn about the different characteristics of children and how to teach them.

Lamentations 2: 11-12 talk of the condition of the people left behind when the children of Isreal were carried into captivity. This situation is the same today in the world. Children roam about the streets nowadays addicted in all sorts of demon – inspired habits such as drug addition, absurd habits etc.

Knowing fully well that the devil was working in and through these things, Jeremiah wept about the situation.

What are you doing looking at many children roaming about the street nowadays? Will you allow them to go to hell? Lamentations 4:3 goes on to draw a sharp distinction between animal and man in this regard.

2

Animals feed their children, but man, alas, doesn't. Do you as a Christian feed your children with the milk of the word of God? Why do you think they easily understand and speak dirty languages you hear them say many times?

The reason is that there is a void in their heart at this early stage yearning to be filled, hence they grab just anything to fill! hence they grab just anything to fill it. For example, a Christian man said he cannot allow his children to leave in a boarding house because the child will be corrupted. No, this is disagreeable. If the Christian has taught his child the way of the Lord, there is no fear the child going to live in a boarding School because he will go there to be a light and change others for Christ by his conduct, testimony and stand.

A pathetic situation is revealed in Lamentation 4:4 Children are spiritually hungry. If in a Church meeting, we just gather them aside only to be told ordinary stories and fables;

So that they may not make noise or disturb the elderly ones, we are making them thirsty. Children, as other human beings have spirits and it is very sure that the soul of a child, man, woman will either go to heaven or hell. No unclean spirit shall enter into heaven. Many children are demon –possessed they can perish. Matthew 18: 1-4 gives us a picture of the concern of Jesus to the salvation of the child.

In Matthew 18:2, Jesus did not look afar to send for a child he would use as example here. He picked one beside him. This implies He evangelized children too. He set a child in the midst of the disciples. In verse 3 Jesus teaches about the little children. Some of their characteristics are that they are humble and reachable. Until we become like them, just as Jesus Himself was, we cannot enter the kingdom of God.

In verse 6 we are told of a truth that can never be denied and that is that children can believe and accept Jesus as Lord and savior. In Acts 16:31 Paul and Silas were admonishing the jailer to accept Jesus Christ and be saved he and all his house including children.

3

If then children are to be save and can accept Christ, then it implies they can perish. Verse 14 further confirm it that they can be saved or perish! Why don't you stand up and do something about this? Verse 10 tells us that just as adult Christians they too have guiding angels. Do you think angels will guide unbelievers? And these same angels look continually into God's face? Heb. 1:14 tells us the kind of people angels guide or minster to. Heirs of salvation only have of the word to them?

If you know they can believe or perish, then you must do something about it.

Does Paul the apostle say something about the children being saved? Yes, he did.

In the introductory verse to Colossians (Col.1:1), we read that the book was writing to saints at Colossians. These are not self-glorified, but it is a fact that if you have received the Lord Jesus Christ even before dying you a saint, In the book written to the Colossians, Paul grouped the Christians (saints) as wives, children, men etc. all saints Col.3:18 is addressed as wives (saints) verse 19 is addressed to husband (saints) and verse 20 is address to children (saints)

He admonished the children (saints) to obey their parents in all things. Why don't your children obey you in all things? The reason is that they have not received the Lord Jesus. Paul was writing to saints (children) so your children will obey you if they become saints. In the later part of Col.3:20 the Apostle Paul proclaims for this is well pleasing unto God.

And if your home is well pleasing unto the Lord, it implies that multiples of blessing will come to your home. What does

God say of Abraham? Gen. 18:19 gives us God's testimony of Abraham. He would command his children and his household after him .and they shall keep the way of the Lord to do justice and judgment. Can this be said of your home? We all known how Abraham was mighty blessed. Jacob and Esau came from the same womb, but God knew Esau would not keep to His way. He knew he would unequally yoke with the women of Canaan.

4

One can imagine him being closer to inherit "the blessing of Abraham "and the Abraham covenant, what evil would that have been? Why don't you teach your children? Are you really obeying what God command about child training?

Paul also addressed the letter to the Ephesians to saints and he had some admonitions for the children saints at Ephesians too Eph 6:1 -3 Although the child training is a joint effort of parents, either of the parents can take it up if the other refuses, mother can take it if the refuses. Timothy was trained in the way of the lord by grandmother (Lois) and mother (Eunice) 2 Timothy 1:5, 2 Timothy 3:14 -15.

Everybody has a role to play in the training. Are you going to give yourself up to be use in this regard? It is not God's will that children should perish (Matthew 18:14) If you are determined you will do it. Don't think you are unable. God is ready to use you! God uses broken vessel.

For example, the roof was broken to let down the man sick of palsy (Luke 5: 18-20 Jesus broke the small bread he receives from a little child, gave thanks and it was multiplied (John 6: 1-14). How many ate of it? The woman with alabaster ointment broke it before the perfume started to give fragrance. (Lk.7:36-38) You also can be broken. You'll be like a clay in the hand of the porter. So, he can break, mold and shape you if you are willing. Now!

CHAPTER TWO

THE WAYS OF EVANGELISING CHILDREN

We have so far considered the Biblical bases we have in evangelizing children. Now we want to talk on how to lead children to Christ. 1 Corinthians 2:14 says may take them for ordinary stories like fables because they understand them as letters and the scriptures say the letter killeth, but the spirit giveth life "Because the child can be taught to his gain, He man must first have the new life of spirit the Lord of God in him through the born-again experience.Also, as a teacher one must first of all have had the new birth experience. In Old Testament only the son of Aaron was Priests. But now we are all priests 1 Peter 2:9.

5

What we ought to do then as priests is to make acceptable sacrifice to God on behalf of those we teach. Hence these lessons are very important. But ask yourself, am I a position to go out and feed these children? I am I well feed too? For Example, as a teacher if you want to release 1,2,3,4 up to 5 you ought to know up to 10. If you want to clothe another person people say, your own clothing first has to be adequate. Before furthering our teachings let us pause to examine our self as living sacrifice. I f you have not accepted the Lord Jesus Christ into your life do it now. You cannot be useful without the new birth experience

CHAPTER THREE

HOW TO TEACH AND LEAD CHILDREN TO CHRIST

During the course of these teachings, we shall learn a lot of songs all the wordings of the songs should be explained to them. Teaching the melody alone will not suffice. For example, there are songs on two of the commonest road signs, STOP, and GO. When teaching the children about the song on STOP for example one can ask them what they will do or what should be done when you are on the road and see a sign STOP on the road. If one does not stop, what happens? Surely if one does not stop one can hit another person. But in our own case, we are going to STOP in another perspective different from stopping on the road.

This time we want to STOP somebody and tell them what the Lord has done for us. He forgives our sins. Then we have to explain what sins are to the children. We can explain that sin is anything that is against the will of God. Remember the day you lied, stole or abused another person. We should then go on to tell them that it was because of sin that Jesus came to the world from heaven, doing good; but many did not like him and so he was taken one day crucified – nailed to the cross, but he rose up the third day to cleanse my soul and make me whole. Teaching the song STOP, which goes like this

Stop and let me tell you

What the Lord has done for me to see.

6

He forgave my sins, and he saved my soul
He cleansed my heart and made me whole
Stop and let me tell you
What the Lord has done for me

CHAPTER FOUR

HOW TO LEAD CHILDREN TO CHRIST

There are four important things to note of in this regard:

1.Let the child see his or her need no punctuation to receive the Lord Jesus and Savior. Let him know that not everybody is going to heaven, and that the Lord Jesus Christ came to make those who receive him go. But because of man's evil deeds, he cannot. The Bible says there is none righteous, no not one! (Mathew 19 :17) Therefore there must be someone to save man from his evil deeds. Therefore, the child is made to realize he needs Christ to save him from his evil deeds and hell.

2.Explain the way of Salvation very carefully. The teacher must be very versatile in this to be able to explain.

However the way one explains to adults is not the way one will explain to children. For example to an adult audience one can define sin as "transgressions of law "but to the child, this may be very difficult to grasp. One way of explaining what sin is will be to ask how many of the children have ever been beaten by their parents. Many will surely rise up hands. One may then go on to ask whether they were beaten for doing something good. They will surely say no, and that what they did was something wrong, and that was why they were beaten by their parents then"

Then explain that the wrong they did were example of sin. One can go further to explain the way and that because of sin one cannot make heaven. Explain further the way of salvation. Make heaven. Explain further the way of salvation.

7

Explain further the way of salvation. Make clear that it is the only way without which we cannot get to heaven.

- Tell them the decision to be made and the acceptance of the Lord Jesus Christ as Lord and Savior

- Give them the basis to receive assurance of salvation and eternal life, Then what are the means or methods of bringing this child to the Lord Jesus Christ

a. Gospel Glove- with colors won to explain the way salvation

b. The Wordless book – having five different colors on the pages used to explain the way of Salvation love

c. Gospel Nuts – having same colors in (b) above

d. In the class we can use different pictures to illustrate. In the absent of pictures, illustrations can be made with the fingers of the hand. The five fingers denote the five steps in leading the child to Christ. They can also be taught on explain with their own hand **GOSPEL GLOVE**

Using five different aids in conjunction with the Gospel, the explanation will be something like the followings.

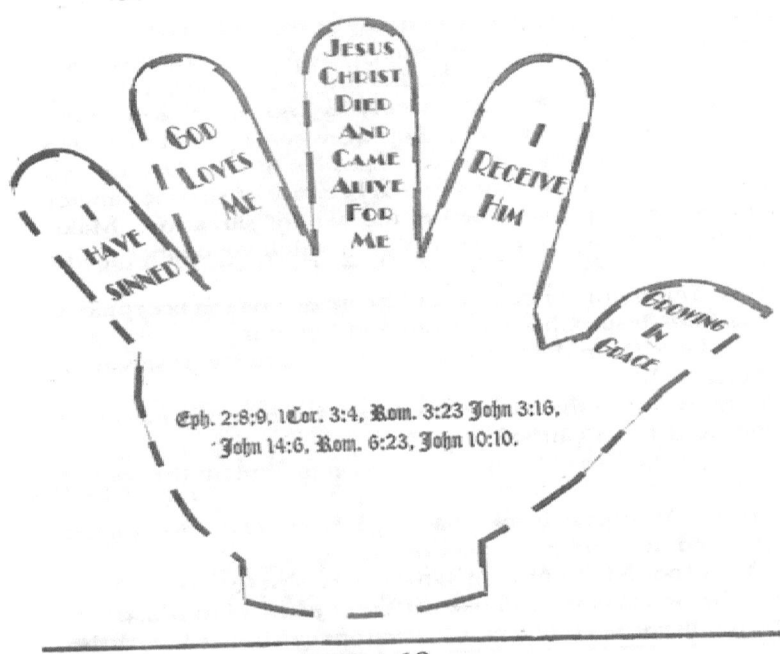

10

GOD LOVES ME: The children can be asked to put in their names e.g., God loves John! The Bible says Jesus is presently preparing a place for us.

Heaven is a wonderful place, even the streets are of gold.

Ask the Children, Do you know gold?

Ask the Children; Is it something you can see all about?

Ask the Children, Does mummy have gold?

Ask the Children, Does she keep the gold in the kitchen?

Ask the Children, Dose she keeps it in the gutter or trash can around the house?

Or does she hide the gold somewhere safe?

Gold is precious, is usually kept very well in a safe. But that's what we are going to walk on in heaven right on the street of heaven! Because of the love of God for us. There will be no crying there.

Ask the Children, how many of you have cried before?

But in heaven no crying will be there. There will be no sickness in heaven!

Ask the Children, how many of you have been sick before? In heaven there will be no sickness over there, because God love us.

But do you know one thing that is not in heaven? The Bible says all have (I HAVE) sinned and have come short of the glory of God (Rom 3:23) All we like sheep have gone astray……It is sin. Sin will not be in heaven.

Remember the day your teacher asked you to do some homework or something, but you did not do it, but you told the teacher you did it. That is a lie. That is a sin, and it will not be in heaven. Remember the day mummy told you to put a tin of milk in the refrigerator and just before putting it there you sipped a little bit of it and covered back before putting it back in the refrigerator.

That is sin. If you sin you live in darkness of sin so you cannot get to heaven, but the good news for you is that Christ died for you. Do you want to tell us some things He did?

(The children will give different answers) then make them understand that not everyone will make heaven and that not everyone on earth love Jesus Christ. So those who did not like Him gathered together conspired and killed Him nailing him to the cross. If a man is nailed to the cross what comes out?

(The children will definitely say blood) Then explain further that Blood that takes away sins. The Bible says "Without shedding of blood there is no remission of sin "(Hebrew 9:22)

He has died for you. Will you call Him into your life so that He can wash all your sins away? Will you then receive the gift of salvation? He is offering. You can receive the gift with a hand of faith. Jesus stands at the door of your heart knocking. If any man —male, female, child, adult will open the door of your heart to Him. Jesus will come inn...... Do you want to open the door of your heart to the Lord Jesus today? The hand of faith receives gifts from God. Do you want to receive this free gift of salvation? He is ready to give you NOW, Receive it.

If you receive this gift of salvation, then you will be saved and then you will be able to go to heaven where the street is made of gold. Where there is no pain, sickness or sin, but joy and where we shall be forever with the Lord Jesus Christ,

Notes: Note the sequence of the hand glove aid - (a) God loves me (b) I have sinned (c) Christ died for me (d) I receive him (e) I'm saved

It is the power of God through the indwelling Holy Spirit speaking through you that can work and change the heart of these children. The aid s is helpful but where they are not available, not hands are, hence we can make use of them to illustrate.

CHAPTER FIVE

(B) THE WORDLESS BOOK

The wordless book has five different pages of different colors which individually convey the message as the hand Glove aid.

GOLD

BLACK

RED

WHITE

GREEN

13

Page 1 –GOLD –This talks of the streets of Heaven made of gold, Revelations 21 tells us of the things in Heaven and those things not there, Compare Heaven to the earth. In heaven Christ Jesus will be there, so also the tree of life, angels, etc.

Page 2 - Dark – (None avoid calling this page black, BLACK page, because children are sensitive and such question like "(Whether African being black are bad race etc. will come up")

This page stands for sin, Bring out the sins that children commit (not adults sins) Allow the Holy Spirit to lead you to mention the sins children commit like stealing, lying, disobedience etc.This will lead them individually to see the ugly picture of themselves before going forward.

Page 3. RED PAGE:-The BLOOD – of Jesus Christ .Relate the story of the death and resurrection of the Lord Jesus Christ and "without shedding of the blood there is no remission of sin "Hebrew 1:12

Page 4- WHITE PAGE –Sin washed, after receiving Jesus gift of salvation our sins will be washed away and we shall go to Heaven. John 1:12

Page 5- GREEN PAGE –After we are saved (our sins washed away) we need to grow just as the green grasses and trees we see all about. Here it is important to grow in grace and in the knowledge of our Lord Jesus Christ. The wordless book like the hand Glove tells the whole story

CHAPTER SIX

HOW TO TEACH MEMORY VERSE

Another important thing in teaching children is to let them memories the word of God. The Psalmist said, "Thy word have I hidden in my heart so that I will not sin against you." (Psalm 119:11)

This will help the children to grow in then Lord. It is important to know the particular place in the Bible from which any memory verse is taken. The act of learning memory verse is likened to the sandwich we normally eat. If you want a loaf below the meat and other sources of the sandwich so that one's hands are not soiled. In the same way when learning the memory verses, we say the Bible reference first (loaf) then the recitation of the verse (sauce) and finally we say the reference to top it all (loaf)

It also not enough to teach the memory verse, it is very important to illustrate (say on flannel board) and perhaps more important to let them know the word are right there in the Bible .That is we want them to know that the Bible is the word of God .So one has to read out in their

Presence or allow it is right there .By this word of God is impressed in them. Pictures will help the children to remember what we teach them. If possible use pictures to illustrate the memory verse.

For example Galatians 6:7 gives illustration of deceit. For example a very common example of deceit is the impersonation of man on farms to scare away birds and animals that can destroy crops. A stick is normally clothed to look like man and with probably a hat to match, but as time goes on the arm than ever.

Illustrate (using Galatians 6:7 as an example) and make them understand ways men can be deceived thinking we are deceiving

God. God cannot be mocked. For example a child Evangelist went somewhere re with a boy one day one and left the boy in the carbon coming back he noticed that the marrow has been changed from the passion he formerly put it, the gear changed and other things also put in disarray. He confronted the boy in the car who said he did not know the person who did it .The boy through the Evangelist would be deceived, but he was not. The boy was actually doing all those things at the risk of his life. What if the car moved as he was changing the gear?

The boy later confessed and was spanked. He promised not to do such thing again.

At School, if student does not do his or her homework and assignments and he think he is deceiving the teacher, when the examination comes his fate will be shown everybody to see. Recently, there was a story of a student at a University who committed suicide because he failed his examination. He was not conscious of failure when he was deceiving himself by not studding, and now he reaps the reward of deceit, Example can also be giving of children deceiving themselves thinking they are deceiving their parent's. The result come out.

Different ways of making the children to memories can also be used. Example, may be making those in shorts, those in long trousers, grown wrapper etc. This is to make sure everybody understands thoroughly. Another way of teaching it can be the ping pong method (as if playing, verse one by one alternatively i.e.K.pronounces the first word, J will pronounce the next K comes again to pronounce the one after that etc. At the end they will both recite the memory verse again.

For teacher who knows music, one can always find a song with the memory verse. If you cannot make out a song, give the children a challenge and tell them that when they go home, they should sing and make a song with the memory verse. The child can also teach parent at home as well as other mates.

You may not be an artist, but you can make or do with some sketches which are so useful in reminding children of the memory verse.

A boy was taught what black board is, using the Bible, so whenever the boy is asked he goes to the Bible to remember.

Example of such songs as can be learnt are given below:

Abraham's blessings are mine to see
I am blessed in the morning
I am blessed in the evening
Abraham's blessings are mine

CHAPTER SIX

HOW TO PREPARE A BIBLE LESSON

It is not enough to read to children from the Bible but there is a need to know what to put in a Biblical story or passage to make it a lesson. In any case all scriptures point to the Lord Jesus Christ. Hence there is the need to know what each book, chapter, and verve talk about as well as the theme of such, with a congregation of Children –some will be coming for such gathering for the first time, some for some time while some might have been coming for quite a long time. It is therefore important for all these categories of children so that those that have been coming before will not be bored but progress in the faith. Any story can be divided thus for a lesson:

1. INTRODUCTION: Unless the story is property introduced it will not have enough impact.
   It must capture the interest and attention of the children.

   What are those things to be put in? The introduction should – (a)Capture interest and gain immediate attention (b) Be brief – compared with the body of the lesson (c)Be connected and related to the story (d) Be directed towards the climax which is the highest point of the story. For example, the story of the woman with issue of blood. The climax was when the blood dried up.

2. LIST OF EVENTS: This is a sequence of how the story started and ended. It is picked directly from the Bible. An example is the story of Moses Exodus 1:2 -10

10. The list of events may be something like the following:
(a) How the children of Israel come to Egypt
(b) The new king who did not know Joseph
© How the new king started to ill-treat Israelites

How Israelites multiplied despite ill-treatment
Midwives commanded to kill Israelite's son

After listing the EVENTS look and meditate on where to bring in JESUS, SIN ETERNAL PUNISHMENT etc. If you teach and then towards the end mention JESUS, It is inappropriate. JESUS has to be mentioned very early in the story as well as further in the story. For example, in Exodus 1:2 -10 an example of SIN worth mentioning is when Pharaoh said little children should be killed. Then in the light of this, the children should be told what the Bible says about all of us and about sin. John 10:9, Acts 4:12, Rom. 5:9, Provb 10:19, Provb 14:21, 1 John 5:17, Then, think how am I going to bring Jesus into this? An example of brining in Jesus is by bringing Him as the person who has died for our sins by His blood and that God through the Lord Jesus Christ will shed Blood and that God through the Lord Jesus Christ will save the souls of men if they accept the finished work of our Lord Jesus Christ.

3. CLIMAX: This is the pitch of the story. For example, a good climax in Exodus chapter 2 is when the baby (Moses) was put at the river side. The children will normally want to hear what will happen next because this portion of the story has an element of suspension, hence they will listen as the climax is gradually approached. The daughter of Pharaoh –the very king who kill Israelites' sons –came to the river! – At this time. That's a climax. In some cases, the children might have known the story but if we allow the Holy Spirit to teach through us it will be a different perspective of the story they will listen to. Christ spent 3 days in the grave before resurrection. That will be new to the children. Everybody will want to listen to fact or the other that the Holy Spirit will dish out to them through you. The children also have to be given challenges. For example in the story of Jonas, ask them: How many of you are like Jonah? Do not disperse the children in suspension. You should finish the whole story and conclude too. Although it may not be easy to finish a story e.g., the story of Moses in a day, but the story can be summarized touching cogent parts and necessary conclusions drawn out.

4. CONCLUSION: Necessary conclusion bringing out lesson leant, step to be taken etc. in summary is necessary necessary to round up each story.

CHAPTER SEVEN

SOME THINGS NEEDED TO MENTION OR TREAT WHEN TEACHING THE CHILDREN

Every Bible story can be made to become a lesson. Before teaching the children, the teacher must have an aim.

AIM: The teacher is not to teach for teaching's sake or to occupy the children. It should be more than these. The teacher in drawing up an aim for lesson ought to ask himself what I want to achieve by the power of the Holy Ghost. Then answer is the aim of the lesson.

The teacher must personally know the story very well and should try and go through the scriptural passage for the lesson four or five times, before coming to teach.

The teacher must first apply the truth to himself. It is usually a sad sight to see either a children teacher or Sunday School teacher unprepared adequately and getting to Church on Sunday morning to rush up preparation for the teaching he is taking up that very morning! It is the sad side of the present world that people do not have time for the things of God. Everybody is chasing the wind. The need to pray and study the Bible and open up our hearts to receive from God.

The aim of the lesson should be two folds:

(a) Towards the child coming for the first time and not saved

(b) Towards those who had been coming especially those who are saved, on how to live the Christian life. If you talk of sin and repentance alone throughout the lesson, those children who are saved and know the Lord Jesus Christ, will get bored and may get themselves busy with some other things. On the other hand, if you talk of Christian conduct or say something on witnessing throughout, the children coming for the first time who have not been saved, will not benefit. As the teacher prepares the lesson, he should look at and emphasize sections which will make the Christians to grow and the new ones and unsaved to receive the Lord Jesus Christ.E.g. In the same Moses "story, the two groups of children can be catered for. Despite the maltreatment by the king of Egypt (Pharaoh), the children of Israel were increasing and waxing stronger –because the children of Isreal were children of God – hence an illustration can be made that however the children child is persecuted, hated and ill –treated, he will grow spiritually and physically more and more because God will sustain him.

On the other hand, all the wicked acts of Pharaoh in the story can be used to illustrate sin and then of course mention the Lord Jesus Christ and His atonement Blood as the Holy Spirit ministers

3. MAIN THRUST: What is the passage really talking about? What is the central or message? Whatever it is will be a major point to be mentioned and emphasize thoroughly and throughout the teaching. The main thrust which is usually a single statement will be hammered occasionally throughout the lesson as Holy Spirit prompts.

4. GOSPEL: We have said that the Biblical story alone cannot meet the need of children. What then can? It is the gospel. Hence, we have to weave the story around. The gospel.

What then is the gospel? Paul, the Apostle, said it is "the power of God unto salvation to everyone that believeth "(Rom. (1:16 see also 1 Cor 15:1 - 4) Paul received the gospel and delivered it to people .Verses 3 and 4 of 1 Cor. 15 teach and give complete picture of what the scriptures teach about the gospel, All these elements of the gospel are to be brought into the lesson whether the story is taken from the New Testament or from the Old Testament. All the Prophets knew the promises of Christ the Messiah even from Gen. 3:15. The promise is glaring. Although it took some time to be fulfilled. Therefore, to help us remember what to put as gospel consider the letters of the word Gospel itself one by one in sequence:

(a.) **G - God's love**, Put into your story attribute of God. Look at any lesson you are teaching and bring out how God demonstrates His love to his people. Mention the love of the same God to us as individuals and collectively. Bring out the relevance of John 3:16. Mention also has to be made of other of God such as his kindness, forbearance, power, awesomeness, righteousness, mercy etc.

(b.) **O - Only sinless son of God**

Christ Jesus is the only one who never committed sin Look out a way of bringing in the Lord Jesus Chris. For example, if there is a promise in the lesson, the teacher should point out to the fulfillment. Make a connection to the Lord Jesus Christ as only sinless son of God. On the other hand, if in the New Testament, identify Jesus Christ immediately He is mentioned in the story. A mention and a reference may be made to the founders of all other religions. All the founders are sinners. Only the Lord Jesus Christ was sinless, that is why He is only one who can remove our sin, No other person can Even the child is small, speak to him or her and let them know that Jesus is the only sinless being that has the earth. It should be borne in mind that in mind that no child is too small to learn. Even if it is only Hallelujah he can pronounce, say it to him or her. The story is told of a small child just going to School who first learnt to say "shut up "and came home immediately to say that to his grandmother. What if the child has learnt to say Hallelujah. If children are made to understand the Lord Jesus as the only sinless and son of God they will not be deceived at any stage of their lives into paganism, idolatry, atheism or any other false religion. In USSR for example children are indoctrinated from very tender age by telling them as well as asking them to repeat that there is no God. In this way they become atheist –necked. But thank God for the underground Church God is using mightily in that part of the world now.

(c.) **S - SIN**

To bring in sin into the lesson, look for an act in the lesson which is sinful and the back up with Bible passages. Also illustrate the sins children commit e.g., stealing, if illustration of sin is made to these children, they would have been shown what sin is. The teacher should try to bring out the mention of sin very early in the lesson so that when the precious blood is mentioned later the Holy Spirit would have used the mention sin to convince the child to make him see the helplessness which no doubt will make him embrace the precious blood. The teacher should be well versed in the scriptures to distinguish between Christianity and other religions. The Christian region is religion of life. In other religions those they believed on died and we can still see their tombs and grave today, but the Lord Jesus Christ resurrected from the dead, triumphing over death and the grave; death could not hold the Prince life –and the savior, the only one who can give life now and after death.

(d.) P – Precious blood

It will be very nice to bring in, the precious blood of Jesus into the story at the early stage, so that the children will know that it is only the precious blood of Jesus Christ alone can bring back sinners to God some Bible passages can be used for explanation of the preciousness of the blood. Matt 26:28, Acts 20 :28 Rom. 5:9, Heb. 9:14, 1 Peter 1:18 -19, 1 John 1:7, Rev. 1:5, 5:9 :7 :14, 12:11

(e.) E - Everlasting

The children most also be made to understand that the blood is still following and that the blood that was shaded on the cross can save you. The blood is everlasting, this also must be considered important to mention to children at the early stage of your message.

(f.) L –Let Him In

This is a kind of invitation. A lot of people witness beautifully but will round off without inviting the people to "Let the Savior in "the teacher has done very little. The preacher or teacher should bear in mind that he cannot effectively make this invitation without completely relying on the power of holy Spirit.

In making this invitation the teacher may try to rehear SIN, JESUS death and RESURRECTION. This will further buttress the gospel. If the children do not know how to pray, teach them and allow them to pray aloud so that one may hear what they are praying for. This is Particularly needful for those that have not receive the Lord Jesus Christ.

CHAPTER EIGHT

1 KINGS 21:1 -20 AS A BIBLE LESSON

As a teacher one must read the Bible lesson for about three times or four times before going to the class to teach. Mark and note whatever is being said of God.

(a) Verse 19 –teaches that God rewards every man according to his work. It whatever a man sows that he will reap. Ahab and Jezebel without having the thought of God as a rewarded of every man's deed, but God repaid them in their own coin.

(g.) Verse 18 – 19 reveals an attribute of God that He is all knowing. Nobody can hide himself in a secret place and will not know. He fills the heaven and earth (Jer.23:24) we should talk of God as the God of Judgment as well as love. The two are inseparable attributes of God while man is still alive should be mixed with the flour if we want to use it to make bread from the very outset, in the right combination, not after mixing the flour. In the same way one should not finish the story before starting to talk about attribute of God. We should mention all attributes of God we can find in the story along throughout the story.

Recall that we weave any Biblical story around the GOSPEL, in order that deep rewarding spiritual facts may be drawn out to meet the need of children. The Lord Jesus Christ had to be brought out in a natural way into the story.

G - We have talk above of an attribute of God –love tied with judgment. Next, we consider how we can bring in the Lord Jesus Christ as the only sinless son of God.

O - Only sinless son of God. Naboth in this story is a type of Jesus Christ. He died without a cause for dying. He did not do anything wrong to Ahab and Jezebel before being killed for no offence, He was the only sinless son of God. Apart from the above figure or type of the Lord Jesus Christ an offering should be brought out as picture of later reoccurrence. The Lord Jesus Christ offered himself once and for all. The people of Old Testament sacrificed when they sinned, but Christ offer Him once and for all. If it is prophet who is one of the main characters of the story, bring out the relevance especially as related to the Lord Jesus Christ, how for example.

According to Gen. 3:15 it was prophesied He would conquer and utterly subdue Satan.

S – Sin Mention should be made that God is the God of love and justice. Sin must be mentioned early in the lesson so that the child can lean easily and relate it whenever he hears the Lord Jesus Christ mentioned. You cannot just stop somewhere he hears the Lord Jesus Christ mentioned You cannot just stop somewhere and start to talk about sin. Look at the passage and bring out sinful acts of the characters. Such examples in our text include the Following.

(I) Ahab went to Naboth to ask for his (Naboth's) vineyard, He was refused. He went home dejected Why? Ahab was covetous. Ahab wanted his own way. This is a picture of sin.

(II) Jezebel's evil counsel and plan to get rid of Naboth.

(III) Naboth was kills, Always look very early in the passage for a place you can talk of sin. As we look and bring our sins, we must choose and bring out Bible passages to support. Such may include passages as Isa. 53:8, Rom 3:10 etc. after that go out to apply the truth to the i.e., that have sinned and come short of the glory of God. Let this be very clear. Avid saying "everybody "in pointing out sin, always personalize it to the child by saying "you" to the child. If you use a general language some will excuse themselves. After this bring out the examples of sin. In bringing out the example of sin.

In bringing out the examples of sin allow the Holy Spirit to lead you into mentioning those sins which are common to them to their age group. Examples of such sin may be a kind of thief whereby when a child's parent told him to go and f each sin clearly. Up again before putting it the refrigerator. Another example may be abusing people etc. always use example to bring out the meaning of sin clearly. This will allow the Holy Spirit to convict a child of whatever he been doing. (It is a pity most teachers do not sit down and think through the lesson they want to teach and allow the Holy Spirit to talk to them. Our lesson is centered on the word of God and of course on reality. Actually, happened so think through even including the events likely to have happened at the background e.g.

Ahab like the king he was, might have gone to Naboth's place in full pomp and pageantry so that he would command respect and Naboth would have panicked because of that panicked and give his inheritance (his vineyard) to Ahab the king. In this way the teacher and the children will be blessed as the Holy Spirit gives unction. Endeavour to plant the picture of the lesson into hearts by acting us under the direction of the Holy Spirit what action out under the direction of the Holy Spirit what actions would have taken place and how, for example, Ahab was actually wealthy and has vineyards too and upon all he was the king. So, an illustration of Ahab coming to Naboth to ask of his vineyard (Naboth's) with the authority of a king over his subject (which Nabot was) can be made. The Holy Spirit will use this type of demonstration to minster the truth of the story, most often, teacher's complain they do not picture aids, but most of the picture aids we use are ideas thought of and painted by some other people. Hence, we also can thing for example of how we can bring up some pictures from a lesson.

As you prepare your lesson make preparation on how to make your own picture too.

P - Precious of Jesus. Christ Point out Biblical reference like 1 John 1:7, Heb. 9:22 etc., that talk of the blood of the Jesus Christ as the atonement for human sins Then mention or tell a short story of the death, and burial of the Lord Jesus Christian and then connect P (Precious Blood of Jesus Christ) to E (Ever living Savior) to talk of the resurrection and His presence at present the right hand of God the father interceding.

E - Let the children understand that the blood of Jesus is ever living (still flowing) and if they can submit themselves, by faith they could be washed in the blood.

L – Let Him in. This is the conclusion of the message as you invite the children to take decision and allow the savior to come in their hears. To fully buttress this point reference used. Examples of each reference are. John 1:12, John 3:16, Acts 16:31, Rev. 3:20 etc.

COUNDITION: Believe in the Lord Jesus Christ.
PROMISE: You will be saved…

Explain the condition and promise, and then ask them if they want to take the decision and let the Savoir into their hearts.

You can then ask those that are ready to take the decision to stand up or join you in front or remain in seat while others go out. Then have the children properly counseled. If they have not fully grasped all what has been said, repeat the message as concise as the Holy Spirit leads. This is especially for the children who are finding it difficult to take decision, but for those who have given up their lives to the Lord, challenge them to live a holy Christian life

Many of the things enumerated above apply to the child that has not been save.

What then are those things that ought to be included for the saved ones? What are the things revealed in the passage (1 kings 21:1-20) that a Christian should not do or should emulate?

CHAPTER NINE

CONVETOUSNESS

This is quite common among children. It may be that at the Church for fellowship the child has seeing that other children change dresses quite often, some buy pretty new ones and some do not wear a clothe twice. The child may feel covetous and challenge his/her own parents too that they should buy her clothes so that she can dress like these other children. This is covetousness and it is a sin. Ahab in the lesson here was not satisfied with the things he had .Ask the "Are you like Ahab"? If you have received the Lord Jesus Christ into to your life you should always obey God and your parents without grudges.

If the Children that have been saved are treated this way, they will not feel bored that the teacher is talking of sin alone.

In this lesson we can put O.P&E together likewise G&S, and finally in rounding up with L- (Let him in). We see Ahab here after the killing of Naboth that instead of

Then turning to the children the teacher can challenge, Do you want to continue in your sin? Jesus died and arose for you and He is alive today and wants to live in your heart. Then use a conditional promise like John 1:12, works .John 3:16 or Acts 16:31.

Even though pictures are actually very valuable, but it is through man that the Holy Spirit

CHAPTER TEN

CHARACTERISTIC OF CHILDREN

A farmer must know the type of soil he had on his farmland, the type of crops that will grow on each soil type as well as the season when to plant and reap each type of crop. If the farmer does not know, the season to plant and he plant during a wrong time season, the crop will not grow .Foe example , October is the month yam is planted and for a farmer to have planted in August is sheer waste as there will be no yield . In the same vein as teachers we must know the word of God. We must understand the children. One cannot expect that because the children who are saved have accepted Christ then they should behave like adults. Even adult when converted are not changed physically, it is only the heart is changed, same goes for children. For example, children are full of activivities as distinct from adults and no attempt should be made to change them from this direction, since that is the stage of life they are.

As teachers and parents however we need to plan all their activities for them. Distinct time should be planned for eating, talking, playing etc.Twins (includindividuals and be known as such. If you are in the home, you must know how to treat each .Likewise in the fellowship or children class .In dealing with children there are quite a number of basic things to take into consideration.

The basis of our study on the child will be found in Luke 2:52 "Jesus increased in wisdom, stature, in favor with God and man"

There are four important things here:

(a) Wisdom (B) Stature (C) Favor with God (d) Favor with man

The four major traits can be classified thus:

Favor with God.................................... Spirituality

Favor with Man ....….... Sociability

Stature...Physical growth

Wisdom...................................…...Mental Capability

The teacher and parent need to observe and tailor these traits in the children, to fit God's perfect plan for them. All the above-mentioned traits seen in the Lord Jesus Christ should also characterize the Christian child. The children are grouped in the following age range.

Birth ------3 years

4 -----------5 years beginners

6 -----------8 years

9 -----------11 years

12 ----------adulthood

CHAPTER ELEVEN
THE FOUR CALLS OF JESUS

Read: Philippians 3: 7-16

When Jesus was on earth, He called people to come to Him and follow Him. It is a wonderful thing to know that he is still calling people today. and He is calling you by name .He not only calls you to come to Him for Salvation , but He also call you to move onwards and upwards the goal for which He has saved you (Philippians 3 :14 "

In the Great commission the main command Jesus gave His disciple s was to "go and make disciples. This was His call for them and it is also His call for you .The following picture or model will help you see clearly the whole pattern and this disciple making process that Jesus id calling you to be a part of:

READ: Philippians 3:7-16   Memorize: Philippians 3:14

behind and reaching forward to things ahead

When Jesus was on earth He called people to come to Him and follow Him. It is a wonderful thing to know that He is still calling people today and He is calling you. He calls you by name. He not only calls you to come to Him for salvation, but He also calls you to move onwards and upwards towards the goal for which He has saved you (Philippians 3:14).

In the Great Commission the main command Jesus gave His disciples was to "go and make disciples". This was His call for them and it is also His call for you. The following picture or model will help you see clearly the whole pattern and plan of this disciple-making process that Jesus is calling you to be a part of.

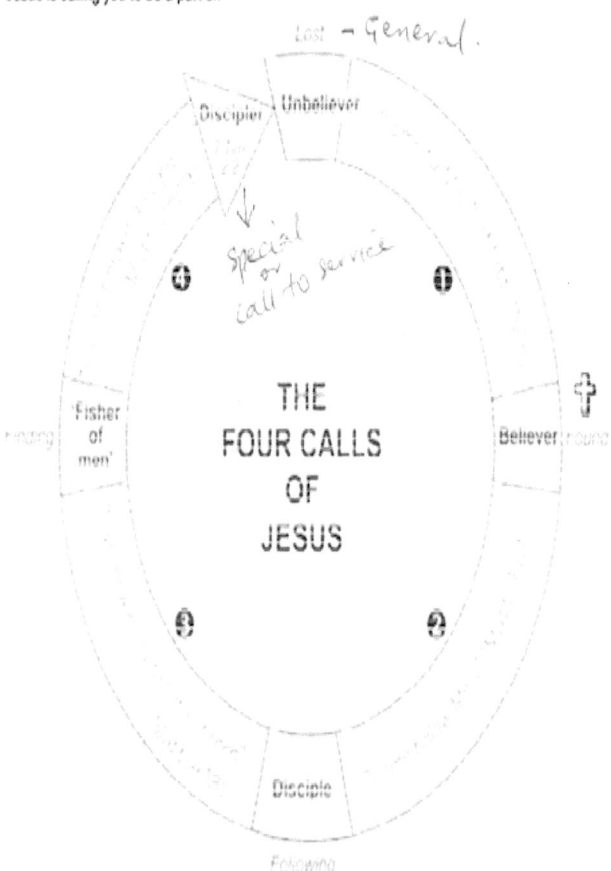

Figure 1. The Discipleship cycle

In this drawing we see four calls of Jesus. Each call is to bring us into closer fellowship with Jesus first of all, and then into a closer partnership with Him in the work of His Kingdom.

13

Four calls of Jesus

1. First call Unbeliever to Believe –We start at the top of the circle with the "unbeliever "who is "lost "from fellowship with God. At one stage you were in this position, But Jesus came "to seek and save you the lost (Luke 19 :10) He calls to those who are wearied and burdened with life, Come to me. Your burden of. Lay down your heavy burden of sin and I will give you rest {Mathew 11 :28}

2. He never gives up until the lost are found and brought back safely into the Father's arms. When a person hears the call of Jesus and believe and comes to Him in repentance and faith, that person becomes a "believer "and a child of God. That person receives God's forgiveness and changes from being lost to being found .Have you heard and responded to this first call of Jesus.

3. Third call: Disciple to Fisher of men
    When Jesus first called those early fishermen with the words "Come follow me "He also told them His purpose with the words "and I will make you a fishers of men " Just as Jesus reached out to you and found you when you were lost , so He wants to train you to become a part of this same process of reaching out to other lost people and bring them to Him also. This is still a part of being a disciple. You will always be a disciple and a learner of Christ right to the end of your life. But as part of following Jesus, He wants to put when you the desire to go and find others that you can bring them also. Do you want to be a part of helping another person come to Christ? This is the third part of Jesus' call upon your life.

4. Fourth call: Fisher of men –to Disciple – maker
    Perhaps you thought that to bring a person to Christ is the end of the line. Well, it isn't! Jesus final call and command to His disciple was not just to "go and make converts, it was to go disciples "{Matthew 28:19 - 20} of course this will mean first of all witnessing, evangelizing and leading people to Christ. But it must go beyond that. There are many people who have been brought to Christ. They have become believers, but they are having not become disciple because they have never properly

disciple. They have been left to find their own way. As a result, many have only gone so far, and remain weak, immature and often ineffective Christians

In 2 Timothy 2:2 Paul urged young Timothy with this word: "The things you have heard me say…entrust {or teach} to faithful men who will be able to teach other too also Christ and follow Him as a disciple. You are then called to go and disciple others in the same way. Doesn't just be a disciple! Become a disciple maker! Learn how to multiply and reproduce spiritually in this way the process continues and multiplies. Isn't a simple and

The Purpose of Sunday school

Why do we need Sunday school in our Churches today? Sunday school is luxury, Sunday school is time waiting, says one Church man, "No I have stopped attending "

There are a few of the questions asked or opinion expressed by a lot of people, even in evangelical circles today, why then does the Sunday school exist?

In any evangelical Church, the purpose is (or should be) twofold: Evangelical and edification: Gal 1:28, Paul sets these objectives out very clearly, "We proclaim Jesus "admonishing every man, warning every man. (That is evangelism) teaching every man, instructing every man, (that is edification) that we may present every man complete in Christ."

- **A.Evangelism**: In the great commission, Christ commanded His disciples to go and preach the gospel to every creature "Mark 16:15" The Sunday School exists to s to obey this great command through winning souls to Christ. By evangelizing, the Church not only increased the population of heaven bound pilgrims, but its numerical strength grows

- **B.Edification:** After souls have been won to Christ; the fruits need to be conserved with a view to developing them into mature Christians. It is not in the best interest of a Church to neither have a large population of members who lives neither glorified nor honor the Church as a community, through wholesome teaching of God's word. The member can develop after their Sprit endorsed gifts and be more useful to God and to one and another. This diagram illustrates the purpose of the Sunday School…Evangelism…Edification emphasizes either one to the… (Numerical growth spiritual growth)

Both of these goals must be held in balance. To emphasize either one to the exclusion of the other is unbiblical, in nutshell, therefore:

The purpose of the Sunday school is to lead people to know God as revealed by Jesus Christ (not only to know about God) and so to love Him and desire to serve Him all their lives.

What should be our objective?

I believe that a very good Sunday school will have definable objective which can be reviled from time to time.

- **Evangelism**

The Sunday school should attempt to win as many souls as many as possible to Christ, by simplifying the gospel massage so that people can understand the implications of accepting or rejecting Christ. Someone has opened that if the gospel message were made much simpler to understand, an appreciable proportion of those who reject Christ would not have done so, I agree with this.

2. Efforts should be made to increase the numerical strength of the Church through personal and mass evangelism. A goal should be set regarding the percentage of growth the Sunday school intends to achieve annually, this goal should be met realistically and appraised, say quarterly and efforts should be geared up where the actual performances falls below the objective.

3. New comers should be visited regularly, prayed for and counseled and made to feel welcomed in the Christian Community so that they will stay until (and after they are saved)

Edification

The believer can be built up spiritually through:

- **Knowledge of the Bible: In** Psalms 119 David said, Thy Word have I hidden in my heart, that I may not sin against thee. The student should encourage to memorize important Bible passages which can be recalled when facing the adversary. Jesus used the phrase "It is written "four time when he was tempted by the Devil in the Wilderness, Matt.4:4,6,7,10

- **Besides memorization :** the students would also know much facts as who was Adam,Elijah,Paul etc.which book of the Bible are in the old and new testament respectively, why Israel split into two Kingdom after death of Solomon, in what chronological order the Pauline apostles were written etc.The the students should also know the major themes and doctrines of the Bible, e.g. the sovereignty of God, redemption, justification, sanctification, the trinity, the life and teachings of Jesus Christ, Heaven and hell, Second coming of Christ etc.

- **Obeying the Lord and His word: The** Student should be encouraged to obey the Lord and His word, the teachings of the word are not meant to be learnt alone but to practice. And we as teachers should lay good examples for them to follow, hypocrisy in whatever form should be avoided at all times." An ounce of example "says an old adage "Is worth more than a ton of money, do not go to work on Sunday to do an optional overtime, instead of teaching them

- **Developing Biblical Attitudes: Effective** teaching should encourage students to change their value system and develop Biblical attitudes." When Paul writes to his friends in Christ at Philippi, "For God is my witness, how I yearn for you all with the affection of Jesus Christ" (Phil 1:8) He was revealing an attitude, When Jesus blessedness those who hunger and thirst for righteousness "(Matt.5:6 RSV.) he is talking about what is basically an attitude towards God......casting all your care upon him "Fear not little flock "be ye kind one to another, tender –hearted, forgiving one another, be ye kind to one another, tenderhearted, forging one another, blessed are the merciful, and trust in the Lord 'are only a few of the many Scriptures which urge us to adopt certain attitudes. The teacher should encourage the students to trust in God whatever happens. For instance, it is not enough to read about the faith exhibited by Abraham when God called him out to an unknown destination. What would be the student's reaction if, as an evangelist, God called him to minister in a village which lacks basics amenities, like pipe –burns water, electricity, good feeder road, etc.

- A student has leant nothing if he still bears his burdens alone. After reading God's advice to us to can't all our cares upon him. This aspect in teaching is very important, because intellectual assimilation of Bible truths or God's promises will not help unless they are applied to real life situations

- The Sunday school should aim at providing an atmosphere conductive to worship (praising, honoring glorifying God) meeting together to edify, encourage, exhort, assist one another} Furthermore, the Sunday school should encourage people to the use their spirit endowed gifts to the glory of God and the benefit of mankind.

SUNDAY SCHOOL ORGANIZATION

The Bible says, "Let all things be done in order "God Himself has set the example for working in an orderly way, when he wanted a nation to honor Him, He first organized the Children of Israel who had left Egypt as multitude of free slaves.

Moses was chosen as leader, and the people were divided into tribes and giving their own places. A written law was provided to guide them. All the works of creation we see around us shows a carefully plan and organization. As the Sunday School is also the work of God, we should not expect it to develop just by chance. We must know what we are doing and then set about to do it in an orderly way.

There are many terms that are commonly used in the Sunday School that must be well understood. As Schools always have classes, the Sunday School has classes that are known by certain names. Classes are divided according to age groups, and even the smallest Sunday School should have at least three divisions.

The Adult class, the youth and The Children

The Children is from birth to about twelve years of age, the period of childhood is usually divided into the time before Child is old enough to go to School and after he began School. These two divisions may be divided again from birth to when they are expected to learn much (three years of age) but the little ones cannot be expected to learn too much as he is too young. But nevertheless, he should go, and when he is old, he will not depart from it. Says the Scripture.

Such training should begin even before the child is old enough to understand what is going on. The cradle roll or nursery class has been prepared for him. If at all possible; the Sunday school should provide a place for the nursery. If the little babies can be kept together, they will not disturb their mothers or older brothers or sisters who may have to take care of them. Several good women can be appointed to watch over the babies and keep them happy. It is good to have roll of babies, and as soon as a new baby is born the person in charge of this class should enroll them, the name, date of birth of the baby. Even baby from unbeliever's home may enroll if the parent gives us permission and this is one of the ways of inviting their parents to the Church. The term used for this little one is cradle Roll.

When babies get old enough to crawl or walk about, they do not like to sit quietly or held by their mothers. Try to provide a place for these little ones and furnish some toys for them to play with. As small as they are, they can begin to learn a few things and good women or more than one in charge of such class can sing then and even in their play direct their little minds towards the things of God. A class of two and three years old can be designated as the nursery class or infant class.

After a child reaches the age of four, he can begin to learn many things; He is old enough to go to a class in Sunday school and has simple Bible stories and Choruses taught him. He has not yet been to School, so as he cannot read, but he can learn by what he sees, object lesson and visual aid materials are helpful to this age, together with five years old, these Children can form the beginner class,

Six years of age is the time that a child usually enters School. In School he learns how to play with Children, and he must also learn to get along with them. Before this, he has probably done such as he pleased in his own home, but others of his age will be there and challenge his right to please himself.

He is just learning to read, and this opens a new door to him. Even in area where children do not have the opportunity of going to School, they develop new interests at this age and therefore should be separated from the beginners. The primary class is thus made up of children of 6, 7 and 8 years of age.

The next age group is very important, up until this time Children will usually accept what they are told, but now they begin to ask more questions and think for themselves, they become more conscious of the world around them. Adult and uninteresting Sunday School will not hold them. Therefore, it is important that these 9, 10 and 11 years of age, whom we call the juniors, be given careful attention.

At about the age of 12 the Child begin to enter a new phase of life. He is approaching puberty, and this brings about an entire change in his body and mind. Because of these changes, he become more interested in the opposite sex. Often the changes bring great confusion to his own mind, and this age group needs special understanding and oversight. This intermediate class is formed for the 12,13 and 14 years old.

Those 15, 16 and 17 are approaching manhood and womanhood, during these important years young people are often lost to the Church. They find a great interest in the things of the world. Sin is attractive to them. They do not like the people's reproach, and they are offended when others of their age laugh at them and mock at them going to Church. The Sunday School has a great opportunity of holding these young people steady, but much preparation is needed.

From 18 to 24 the characterization of this is not so different. This is the time of activity and your people whose activities can be channeled into the things of God can be greatly used. It is also the time responsibility to a great temptation, and the Sunday School has a special responsibility to provide a solid foundation that will hold them steady during the storms of testing.

From the age of 24 a person is considered grown up and so becomes a member of the adult division, Adult can be divided as necessary because of numbers, but there is no special division other than that. It is often wise for Women to have their own class, as some of them will not take active part when men are present.

The other group of people most considered, there may be some in your town who cannot come to Sunday school because of sickness or old age, we must take the Sunday school to meet them in their home or sick beds.

Exciting plan? And God is calling you to be a part of it.

www.ingramcontent.com/pod-product-compliance
Lightning Source LLC
Chambersburg PA
CBHW050906120626
46554CB00003B/1045